Lie Detection: Develop An Eye To Spot A Liar & Never Be Deceived Again!!!

Aiden Mccoy

© 2015

Disclaimer

Table of Contents

HOW TO DETECT A LIE: Develop An Eye To Spot A Liar & Never Be Deceived Again!!!

Aiden Mccoy

© 2015

Steps to Becoming lie proof

From the finest to new age, this book introduces modern lie detection tactics used by the best of in the field of lie detection and how to uncover them, there are well arranged chapters applicable and fun to read, un ravel all the mysteries , myths and facts of the liar, know their weakness and gain an advantage over them.

Introduction to how to detect a lie

Lying is an art. It is a lifestyle to most and to some, a way of making ends meet, a lie being a false representation in form of phrase or statement that is made with the intention of misleading, the person who is making this false statement is in turn known as the liar or commonly known as the cheater, dating back to B.C it is believed to have begun with the early human beings, first practised by ancient kings and heads of states then moving on to any age group that ever was. It is also known as cheating; there are different myths about cheating from different communities in the world and religion. Statistics has proved that the more we are heading to the next century, the more liars are becoming more skilful and crafty in lying. It is therefore essential to keep up with the pace of identifying lie in the statement for the sake of your well-being or livelihood.

Lying has become a temptation ,it has proved to be unavoidable time after time, Most people could even argue that the truth does not actually set free and that it's more like a plague, it sweeps away the whole field just like a wild fire does to the forest, it does not choose whether young or old, big or small. In this we can justify that many people are drawn, for example we have either read about it or learnt about it from the best of kings and queens, politicians, religious leaders, athletes, families, and children.

Have you come across or maybe had some metal detectors used on you? You probably have while at the mall, airport or a high security detailed building, noticed how those detectors are able to detect any form of metal that you have be it keys or just your buttons? That is exactly how you will be alert of lies coming into your way, by reading this book you will be getting to know more of the foundations of a liar and how to know their pillars. It's a fun journey that gives you the knowledge or rather power to read in between the lines and emotions of different characters.

As we proceed to the chapters you will learn more about how lies have made impact in history and also the various effects that lying has both physically and mentally, the book has been made as reader friendly as much as possible and fun to learn, brace your mind for the thrill of a lifetime as we discover new ways to detect a lie.

THE IMPORTANCE OF MASTERING LIE DETECTION TECHNIQUES

Lying is a negative part of life that has affected all walks of life from the rich to the poor, all races, politics, religion, and the whole world in short. We have either learnt about lying from divorces, politics and even myths but have you ever known that you can actually tell when a person is lying to you? And not forgetting that being misled has led to larger consequences that lead to legal action? During the historic times the inhabitants had instilled enormous punishments for victims found guilty of lying, lying was considered a capital offence, a victim found guilty would either be sentenced to hanging or being fully burnt alive, from the greatest of king Richard the third who was punished by harsh beating to Bill Clinton who was found guilty of having an affair with a young woman working in the white house to Tiger Woods who was also caught red handed cheating on his wife have all faced the music as a result. Take a moment and imagine if you were the culprit in those cases, all the lies you believed were true would now be uncovered, how would your physical and mental reactions react? I bet there would be mixed reactions, feeling angry and at some point wishing bad luck to be fall the culprit. Well, you don't have to worry anymore of being the victim, Join me as I go through the book unravelling and discovering new ways of exposing lies no matter how hidden it might be or simple as a leaf.

I. Myths about a liar

A myth is said to be a story that has been passed down from ancient time with the main aim of explaining what, how or when something or an event takes or took place, it also incorporates either humans with supernatural abilities or abnormal powers.

A myth about a liar is simply how the liar came into being, there are lots of believes on how the liar came to being or rather how to detect the liar, some myths include.

a.   Somebody is a liar if they don't maintain eye contact with their audience

b.   Somebody is a liar if their heart beat rate increases as they are conveying a statement

c.   Somebody is a liar if they make suggestions that only reflect upon their interests

d.   A liar will often be the first to object or suggest opinions in a case

e.   A liar will cross his fingers or legs or maintain a crossed posture while telling the lie

f.   The ears of the liar will turn red since telling of lies heats up the ears.

There are more myths about lying than you can ever imagine, ranging from religion to politics to even certain seasons in time.

The origin of the lie

The origin of the lie is not quite verified scientifically even now, there are a lot of explanations but it has never been known which is certain.

Here are some examples of beliefs on origin of lying.

- Christians believe that the very first lie came about when the first humans ever created i.e. Adam and Eve were deceived by Satan into eating the forbidden fruit.

- Other religious beliefs such as pagans, Hindu and Islam believe that lying has come about as a result of greed and cowardly behaviours.

- In the A.T.S (African traditional societies) most communities believe that lying originated from bad ancestral spirits whereby they would lie of a fourth coming event such as rain or drought.

Significance of lies

Some lies were used for the betterment of a harsh rule while others have been used to favour mischief, An example of a lie that was told for the betterment of harsh rule is when Sir William Wilberforce of the United Kingdom was fighting for the abolishment of slave trade, in one of his many failed endeavours was when he together with his team tried faking signatures so as to get their motion passed in parliament.

It is also important to note down why there have been lies in the present or the future times, this is the main part of the material product that the liars' foundation is based on. In general most people have lied in the past or are planning to lie due to such reasons such as:

- A form of escaping punishment

- To get what they are not allowed to have

- To reduce or avoid suspicion of an activity they are undertaking

- To mislead

- To cover up their secrets

- To avoid questioning

Lies have been there since the beginning of time, due to greed, selfishness or pleasing of colleagues, families or any other people along the surrounding environment, in fact it is one of the first negative activities before even stealing. Century after century the liar has not been left behind but has continued to adapt to new measures to hide his foot prints, just as the technological world keeps developing at a pace so does the liar, every day we hear of success conspiracy stories, from hacking of the internet to how national funds have been squandered to high profile celebrity affairs all perfectly executed under a heap of lies.

The liar

So what makes up the liar, how do they manage to pull off their lies in such a professional way? Here is an in-depth focus of the analogy of facts of how, what and where the liars' strengths and weaknesses are:

Strong holds of the liar:

a.   Acting

This is the liars most resourceful asset, liars are good actors, they know what exactly their prey which in this case is the audience need to know or hear to make the show spectacular, In real life actors must pass through vigorous training and repetition to be good performers, they must have the ability to blend and fit accordingly to another character. The same applies to liars they are good in presenting the lie as well as they have mastered their victims anticipations and behaviours.

b.   Creating barriers or objects from the truth

This is one of the ways you can easily tell someone is lying to you. Most liars are prone to use cover up object words such as "I did not take the stuff from the box in the corner". In this sentence there is the use of the object phrase "stuff from the box", this definitely proves that the person knew of what was in the box. Also take into account the affair case of the former American president Bill Clinton, in response to being asked by the court room if he had an affair with the white house young female intern, he answered "I did not have an affair with that lady." The suggestive phrase he used here was "that lady". He already knew her name and this proved him guilty.

c. Eloquent

The perfect liars have their lies well planned out, from descriptions to questions to answering as expected to their victims; they do not get lost in their old words they have every detail backed up with a follow up explanation in case of questions, it is just like you see in advertisements, they are well fluent with giving you the convincing details and also have answers to your questions that are cut-throat meaning that they have no room for more questions.

d. Usage of suggestive words.

These are the words that are often used by some liars which are basically a mixture of a word to prove there is good motive involved like, "to be honest with you" or "truth being told".

e. Have a feeling of confidence

This is probably the number one aspect of the best liar, the best liars are confident when telling lies, this is to avoid any suspicion, just take a look at the sales and marketing personnel, if they advertised in fear then nobody would purchase their products.

f. Memory

Memory is another factor that liars are strong at, they master the lies so well that they always remember it at their fingertips; they remember word by word on how to repeat the lie. If a liar could be asked to repeat what he said severally, he would repeat the same words as said originally without missing anything.

g. Adaptability

Liars have a unique way of changing their emotions as according to the situation they are in, for example in most cases in the court room when things get heated up for the accused they often change their feelings to either start crying or acting like mentally incapacitated so as to evade the case, I also have witnessed personally a cheating partner in marriage lie about where there were the previous night by pretending they are tired due to working overnight. Next after acting this should be amongst the top ten attributes of the liar.

h. Use of gestures

To gain the victims full attention, most liars will use gestures such as body movements or twitching their fingers and in some cases blinking their eyes a lot.

Weaknesses and loop holes of a liar:

After a glimpse at some of the strengths and areas that the liar has advantage over his victim, we can now have a look at some of the weaknesses and areas that the victim might use to their advantage.

a.   Liars avoid eye contact

Especially when it comes to people that really matter to the liar, they will not lie while maintaining eye contact, they tend to have an emotion of guilt and in certain cases when looked in the eye might become speechless.

b.   Repetition of key words or questions

When somebody is lying to you and you ask them a question, they will fast repeat the question as a way to buy some time to make up an answer; they can also prolong a buzz as they are thinking since they are trying to buy some time.

c.   An alert

Just like an unsuspecting felon is caught up by the law, so is the liar, the liar always has his footsteps wiped out but forgets that the victim may find a way to catch up, in fact in history and recent times most of the liars that have been caught have been in alert, this in alert nature of the liar is basically how he gets caught, in most cases red-handed.

d.   Gestures

Liars always leave some evidence behind this may either be facial expressions such as a fake smile, a fake laugh, placing their hands above their nose, talking sideways suggestive eye contact or nervous reactions while portraying the lie such as pen twisting or finger press ups, some other gestures may include; the liar sits in a way that his feet are pointing to the exit

e.   More participative

Liars are always the best when it comes to giving suggestions, they are fully focused on distracting the lie to some other people or even suggesting measures to curb in disciplines.

f.   Voice change

As the liar struggles to convey the message there sometimes is a change of the voice, it can be speed or volume or even the tone, this one is quite rare with young children.

g.   Evidence

This is so far the ultimate and most common weakness that a liar can manage to have especially at this century where evidence can be easily traced.

There are more weaknesses of the liar that can be found anywhere, as human beings each are unique in who they are so is the liar, a liar can be as careful as a chameleon crossing a tree branch while looking everywhere with its compound eyes.

II. Common playgrounds of the liar

The liar just like any other athlete has to have a field to play in, as explained earlier in the first chapter, the liar must be prepared both mentally and physically to tell the lie, this aspect resembles the athlete who also has to train vigorously to perform better on the field. Here are some common areas that the liar works out in.

In 2011 Harold Camping a man who worked as a radio broadcaster for a Christian radio station in the United States of America claimed that the end of the world was on May 21st, due to this, he gained worldwide popularity and a lot of money from donations, his predictions eventually failed despite how he seemed serious, before that he had made an earlier attempt and failed. The donations were not sent back to the well-wishers but remained in his account. His work certainly paid off, he was now among the richest in the world, despite that there are also other characters that are emerging daily, not only the religious side but also other sides; here we shall take into account the top areas where such is happening daily, these are the fields that the liar performs best at.

a.   Marriages

These are the commonest field in the 21st century of most of the liars, from "He or she is my cousin" to "I am leaving for a short business trip," to "I like your family." These are just some of the phrases made each day, in fact statistics show that in the United states of America where the divorce rate is highest, for every wedding done there are three divorces that follow and out of this divorces, each two are as a result of lying. Therefore concluding that ninety per cent of divorces are the result of liars in a marriage

b.   Politics

Politics is also a key field of liars, most of the people involved internationally as politicians have their interests at hand then the rest follow, from ghost projects to corruption and etc. for example to mention a liar in politics take the example of Bill Clinton, he was found guilty of lying that he had not engaged in an affair with the white house intern.

c.   Contractual agreements

These are happening every second worldwide, for every second that surpasses there is a party being cheated to act on a contract, If you look around and conduct some researches on your neighbourhood you will probably find most people have either been involved in lying in their contracts or yet are the victims ,the most common ways into which people are lied to in this area is through insurance agents who lie about policies, also companies whether big or small lie to each other all in the name of reducing competition.

d.   Relationships

Yes I mentioned it, relationships are a basic heaven for liars to get more than they deserve, lying is actually the number one reason why relationships fail.

e.   Examinations

Where are new liars brought up than an examination room? It's an international concern that most people lack confidence in themselves and results to cheating, most Liars are invented from here, and there are always newcomers in this area.

f.   Sanctuaries of worship

Places of worship nowadays are being misused by liars, there are lies flooding in and out that are leading to global problems, the race to get the dollar through mislead has somehow tarmacked in some places of worship. For example Harold camping as explained in the beginning of the second chapter.

g. In the mercies of human beings

"Let not your kindness be your weakness," a common proverb used in English literature but has been neglected, most liars survive on the lies they feed their victims, I personally have helped a handicapped person who later turned out not to be handicapped, there are plenty of such all over the world.

There are so many fields that the liar can perform in, those were just the usual common ones, be alert of such areas and always have your guard on. In conclusion to the fields of the liars, it is important to remember that a lie is formed with the main aim of misleading.

III. Argument on the degree and motive of a lie

To what extent can a lie be verified as enough to be a lie?

Are there some lies that can be justifiably excused as exemptions?

Should different degrees of lies have different punishable acts?

Have you lied with the motive of saving you or your family's welfare?

Have you been lied to and forgiven?

There are a lot of questions that need to be well covered in gaining more knowledge of the lie and the liar in order to be correct and cautious in lie detection, there is an Arab proverb that says that some lies are actually true, I know you're probably thinking hard on how this can be, But did you know that during ancient history lies were used for the benefit of saving or the future? For example in chapter one the brief story of William Wilberforce and his team; Even in some religions there is the mention of a lie that was used to safeguard from harsh rule.

Take into consideration the commonest form of practise that traditional soccer teams used, if a player in team A would be of great talent and contributed to eighty per cent of every victory, then team B will be working on how to get the player sent off the pitch. The same applies to some lies, some are told with the motive of safeguarding from disaster while others are told for mischievous reasons, therefore we can conclude that there are two degrees of lies:

1.   A lie that is meant to mislead to misfortune.

This is whereby the liar is selfish and tells the lie to benefit himself at the expense of his victim. Take for example if a person sells you land with false representation that you dint know off.

2.   A lie that carries a good motive intention.

A lie that is not said for the benefit of one's own self is forgivable, for example the former president of the United States of America apologized on camera about his affair and was forgiven.

Types of liars

Apart from that it is also wise to know the types of liars, as a debate try to think of some people who have either lied to you or you have lied to and try to know the depth of the lie you used in each.

As you argue in your mind, you will come to the conclusion that not all lies that were directed to you or you directed to others are big enough or small enough to undergo the same consequences, the moment you made your very first lie, you had no clue of what you were doing and maybe you got into deep trouble with that, secondly remember when you either lied or were lied to with such a skilful lie that only a master mind would carry out, if you compare the two lies that you have just thought of you will notice that there are two forms of liars:

1.   The non-experienced liar.

This is whereby either the person lying to you or the person you lied to found out about your lie too quickly.

2.   The experienced liar.

This is the master of lying, has gained experience in the fine negative art as he grew up and now has the ability to execute a lie with nobody noticing or takes time to figure out the lie.

IV. Signs of deception

Ever heard of the term "if you think education is expensive try ignorance?" or rather ignorance is bliss"

That applies too in the game of lies; most people will fall as prey as they have no experience at all in interpreting a lie from the truth, it is important and essential to master cheating signs, you never know they can be useful in desperate times, most people don't even realise they have been robbed till they check their stuff.

Signs of deception are the various ways or actions that you can interpret on someone portraying information to you and tell if it is the truth or lies.

A few months back in the year 2009, Brian a college boy boarded a bus on the way back home, he had been funded some allowance by his mother which he had managed to save up for an entire two weeks, he kept the money in a sealed envelope and put it safely in his pocket, he sat down beside a younger boy who kept asking him questions on how his college was, the boy kept showing his enthusiasm to join the college and Brian was comfortable giving information, as soon as Brian reached his stop, he walked off the car and waved goodbye to the younger boy, the bus drove past and was soon out of sight, Brian felt so majestic , he had acted like a professional and answered all the questions superbly, for a moment he highly thought of himself till he decided to check if the money was still there, he placed his hand on his pocket and felt nothing, he checked again and again but the pocket was still empty he ran searched all over his clothes and bag pack but came up with nothing, he stared at the floor and remembered the young boy had his hands crossed and maintained eye contact with him, that's it he had been misled and as a result got robbed.

Most people happen to fall in Brian's category, where their kindness is taken for weakness not forgetting paying heavily for their ignorance, if Brian had a little bit of mastery in reading signs of deception he would have been able to dodge the boy's attempts.

Signs of deception are not something complex and require algebra or math they are simple and only need your eyes and mind to be alert, these signs will point out exactly why not you should choose to not believe in any of the statements being made, if they are positive you will get the result of a misleading statement and will not fall for it, you will henceforth be superior and gain the upper hand from the liar and be able to come back with a counter action, if you master the following signs you will be making a huge step forward where you will play the lying players.

Below is an arranged sequence of commonly used signs of deception:

1.   Facts not corresponding to presentation.

This is the oldest trick in the book especially used by bosses and other people with authority over the others, it involves comparing two things, one; involves analysing the statement the person you are interrogating is making and two; looking at what the person is trying to justify, for example, a person should not tell you that he was late for work because of traffic, yet you passed the route he or she passes and there was no traffic, or another example would be a liar lying of never knowing a victim but his finger prints or may be other possessions are in the victims custody.

2.	Body gestures, these are the best when it comes to getting a quick interpretation result. Even actors know of how their performance is by looking at the audiences gestures , this gestures may include:

a.	Unable to maintain calmness in posture, the liar will not be steady, he will keep leaning and waking from the table or desk, some even stand up and start walking admiring other things in the room.

b.	Body gestures such as being in a crossed posture , Covering the mouth periodically, appearance of a vein in the forehead (happens in rare cases), not maintaining contact with the eyes, constantly scratching behind their neck and forehead, unable to swallow or gulping.

3.   Expressions, these are also widely used in all liars playgrounds, the liar may:

a.   Touch a certain part of his face periodically as assign of easing tension, for example during Bill Clinton's case he periodically touched his nose while giving false evidence a total of twenty six times.

b.   Biting of the lips. Most liars often move their lips and tongue while telling lies.

c.   The fake smile, the fake smile comprises of only the lips smiling but the rest of the face seems frowning.

d.   Delayed nodding after giving out their testimony or answer, a liar will not be able to coordinate facial expressions while at the same time giving their statement, there are two things working on his mind and is trying the best not to mess up.

4.   Prolonged silence after being asked a question, this happens in most cases, the victim is unable to answer for a short period of time since he is making up a lie.

5.   Repetition of the question asked, this shows that the person is not sure of what to say, it also proves that the respondent didn't anticipate for such a question and might tell a lie.

6.   Placing objects between the statement they made, for example as Bill gates referred to Mrs Lewinsky "that woman" in the statement "I did not have an affair with that woman", after answering a question he was asked during his case.

7.   Change in voice is another sign of showing deception. Most liars will change their voice either to a

low murmur or loud voice or even the speed at which they give details, not only that but their tone might also change.

8.   Avoiding physical contact with the person being lied to is also another way to identify deception, the person who is deemed as the liar in this case will keep his head leaned down to avoid any sort of contact.

9.   The person might start placing some items between you and them it may be a ruler, a pen or anything that is near them, they do this as a way of creating an artificial barrier between you and them.

10.   The person under interrogation quickly changes the mood or state of emotions that they are going through, they can turn fragile at once or suddenly break off and start crying. For example if a person seemed cool and collective at the moment the interrogation about who took the keys started , then after the same person breaks down after

being asked whether he was aware that someone had kidnapped the inhabitants child.

11. Moving of feet is another sign of deceit, science and statistics have proved that while standing in an upright position, people will move their feet as a result of questioning.

12. People who are speaking the truth will accompany their statements with gestures at the right timing; they will keep close contact with their audience and show no sign of deceiving by not using gestures, gestures also prove that somebody knows what they are talking about.

13. If the person who is conveying the statement is flawlessly eloquent, that means that he or she has been working and reciting on what to say which may later turn out to be an ocean of lies.

14.   The reactions of the suspect can also be used to prove whether they are guilty, guilty suspects tend to act defensively when asked questions, they have a suggestive behaviour and can even turn violent when answering.

15.   Liars often talk too much even about information that is irrelevant to the information they are asked, for example a person might talk about the whole community when questioned on the status of his house hold.

V. Techniques of catching a liar

Catching a liar is an important activity than it sounds, it is a process that should be carried out with the uttermost seriousness and caution, it is a high risk venture ignoring the truth especially at this time we are living in, there are a lot of technicalities such as the internet, chat rooms, social sites, and so much more things bringing strangers together that people can go missing without a trace and by people I mean young or old adults, terror activities Can happen if the police take lightly the activity of catching a liar, the criminal that was set free after being declared innocent without interrogation can cause a hefty disaster, letting liars walk free might even lead to misuse of resources.

Example of how liars were caught in different communities during historical times

Some communities once believed that to catch a liar an individual would sent to his or her own death trap, this happened mostly when spies from other communities were given the duty of leading their communities enemy into war, for example community A would send their spy to incite community B on attacking community C, community C and community A would either be rivals, so the spies would then be resent to the third community to report the coming attacks and they were later persecuted.

During ancient times the Chinese would catch a liar by questioning the liar as he chewed on dry rice, he would later spit out the rice and if his mouth was found containing rice particles he would be found guilty, they Chinese believed that the stress caused would make the salivary glands in active and the mouth would dry, thus leaving the particles stuck to the mouth leaving the suspect proved guilty.

Over the many decades there has been rapid theories and ways that continue adding up of how to catch a liar, it has not been an easy task coming up with the techniques and scientists and psychiatrists have combined their efforts in finding better ways to catch a liar by using some of the old traditional methods and modern human characteristics.

Catching a liar is more than catching a thief; in fact it somehow ranges to the category of catching a murderer. Some methods of lie detecting include:

a.   Acting as a friend to the liar.

"No man is an Ireland" Even a liar has to look for somebody they can share their trust with, in this method the victim acts a close friend to the liar and shares some discreet information, the liar then gains trust the victim and ends up sharing the lie, this style is best used by police especially when tackling kidnap or drug related cases.

b.   Torture

This act is more of the last option taken when dealing with legal matters or the national security; it involves forcefully obtaining the truth from a suspect by using painful methods.

c.   Use of the polygraph machine

The polygraph machine has long being used since the eighteenth century; it is a machine that uses reactions of activities in the body to figure out whether information interpreted is the truth or not, it resembles the old version blood pressure machine where by a band is tied to your arm but also has some attachments to be stuck on the person being interrogated head, what a specialist in handling the machine uses is reading the graph results that are displayed on paper in form of a graph or in some machines a display, the suspected person is then asked a series of questions periodically as the machine gives output and the machine operator is able to interpret the results.

d.   Questioning

This is an activity that involves the suspect being asked some questions and then verification is done with the evidence at hand, For example if a suspect left his cell phone in an area under investigation and then claims that he wasn't there the evidence will proof he is lying.

e.   Recording

Thanks to modern technology there are a lot of ways in which you can catch a liar; one of the most used technological ways of catching a liar is recording, recording involves capturing footage using a device such as a tape recorder, surveillance camera, cell phones, spy cameras etc... The list is endless. These gadgets record what is happening at a specified time and place; recording can either be visual or audio. This method is currently the best preferred especially in malls, banks and other institutions and businesses.

f.   Listening

Listening helps a lot, you can learn a lot about a person by talking less and listening more, as you listen to somebody you suspect of lying be attentive to changes in information. I.e. The person might try to confuse you since they may lack the ability to convince. Watch out for any changes in voice, any mixing up while accounting an ordeal and giving inaccurate information. Make sure you listen as a lawyer does and if possible try and write out the main points on a sheet of paper, if the suspect makes periodical poses, this could mean he is making up all the information thus lying.

g.   Arrangement of the interrogation area

Whether in an open area such a food court or in an enclosed refinement, on the table try and place some objects such as pens, keys, bags or other relevant items you might find, in case the person starts building some barriers with those items be assured that there are some elements of lies that are being used.

h.   Set a trap

This involves trapping the liar with bait, just like a small mouse is attracted to bait so is a liar, a liar is trapped by plotting the event that he denies to be involved in in another situation, for example if somebody lies about stealing some cash that was left on top of the table or somewhere safe, the victim can know the culprit by putting some more money on the same place, the liar will eventually be attracted to strike the second time.

i.   Ask the unexpected

One common way that the law enforcers are able to prove the suspect is guilty is by asking the expected, for example if a suspect denied passing by the night club the police can ask if the suspect is sure of the information he is relaying. In turn the suspect will be left in confusion which will prove the likely hood of being guilty.

j.   Nero-linguistic programming (NLP)

N.L.P is an activity that helps in determining whether a person is giving the right information by studying the eyes of the suspect as he tries recalling an imagination of an ordeal. This technique is based on the facts if a person is trying to imagine a voice or picture their eyes will roll to the right side, if the individual is right handed, while trying to put the pieces together of an imagination, their eyes will roll to the right, and vice versa for the left handed. If a person's eyes roll to the left then this shows they are trying to remember something heard. This is a simple experiment that you could even practise on somebody; all you have to do is to be vigilant on how your partners eye movement changes.

k.   Change of topic

If there is a sudden change in topic, an innocent person will find it awkward or be confused while trying to catch on. In another case a guilty person will eventually be comfortable and emphasise on the importance of subject change. You can try this with someone you suspect try getting down to questioning first then after the person is surprised enough change the topic, this always works when executed well.

l.   Explanations

Liars have a common characteristic of trying to be detailed to all types of information, they talk to match while explaining and if you lose your attention to what they are saying, they will quickly twist the story up.

m.   No regrets

The best of the liars do not carry any feelings with them; they appear not to be concerned when it comes to the subject matter in hand.

n.   Good actors

Liars are probably the best actors that ever lived they deserve more than an Oscar award for their performance, to be able to perform the lie perfectly and convince their victims is not something to take lightly, a lie perfectly set involves all body parts coordinating.

o.   Participative

Liars are the first to come up with suggestions especially when finding the culprit is the subject in hand, for example while deciding on how to investigate on ways to punish the offender after he or she is caught, the liar gives the best suggestions as a cover up.

VI. Factors that complicate or make the lie detection process impossible.

While facing or trying to solve a situation there are always those factors that make it impossible to make things right, some might be permanently unsolvable while others are temporary.

As the proverb goes "if its half-truth, consider it a complete lie". It is therefore appropriate to know how to get the correct truth in a statement, it is therefore important to know more about the lie detectors challenges and weaknesses so as to figure out areas that will be challenging as you go by the lie detection process, history has proved that the best way to solve modern problems is by going to the root of the matter, we have seen rival nations become friends through this technique of studying the root cause and finding a solution to it, the same also applies in lie detection the more you learn of the past and present challenges the more you will succeed in your efforts.

When it comes to factors affecting lie detection, the liars are often holding the upper hand and trying to make it as impossible as they can for the interrogator to grasp the truth. Not only does this apply to the liar but the lie detector can also complicate his work if he or she does not follow the right guidelines. The right ways procedures of lie detection should be chosen with regards to:

a. The suspect's health

The suspect's health condition is a matter of consideration, some procedures like the NLP (Neuron-Linguistic programming) have different procedures for the right handed and left handed individuals.

b. The suspects age

Different lie detecting procedures vary with ages, a child will not be tested the same way an adult will, and for example a child will not be tested by using the polygraph unless the subject matter is delicate enough.

c.   The matter at stake.

The lie detecting technique chosen for detecting whether an individual is a terrorist will not be the same technique used in checking if a spouse in a relationship is cheating, as much as it is appropriate to know the truth, it is also considered wise to use the best economic technique.

Some of the common ways that make the lie detection difficult include.

1.   If you have a close relationship with the suspect.

A close relationship always gives room for mercy which in turn is not good, as stipulated earlier suspects usually take your kindness and your weakness and will use it as an upper hand to their full advantage. For example let's say the person you are questioning is a close relative and all the odds seem to be going against them, due to human nature you will find it in you to let the case slip.

2. The suspect will not answer to any questions without a lawyer

Not answering a question until the suspect gets a lawyer is actually a right by the law. The person can refuse to talk until a lawyer comes arrives, this happens mostly when the suspect lacks confidence and is doubtful of the answers they might give, this is just one of the best disappointments that you will encounter as an interrogator since lawyers are best in cooking up stories for the benefit of their client, it will therefore make the lie detection process more harder to go through.

3. Uncooperativeness of the liar

The suspect in hand might refuse to cooperate. Such incidences occur when the suspect refuses to do as required or evades interrogation by either hiding or avoiding you as much as possible. For example the suspect might skip key meetings or refuse to be answerable with or without a lawyer who therefore in some cases leads to you looking for a court order which is a process and will take some time.

4. If the subject in hand affects the suspect personally

If the suspect is directly affected by the incidence, for example if the matter in hand is between family members or an affair from one of the partners with solid ground of reason, for instance if a man cheats on his wife because she is barren and has a child with his affair partner, this case might be deemed personal and lie detection would not be preferred.

5. If the suspect has hope in you

This occurs whereby you are responsible for bringing in a suspect into questioning by convincing them to answer questions on the guarantee that you will not take action against the answers they will give, lie detection becomes a difficult task since you are obligated not to expose the liar even when you realise the suspect is lying, lie detection then becomes in effective.

6. If the information you rely upon has been tampered with or withheld

The suspect in efforts to try and keep his record clean will try and tamper with the information he is required to produce or also withhold it, tampering happens when the suspect changes information that would lead to a final ruling be made on during lie detection, tampering can only be proved to be valid if the suspect did it willingly and with the motive of misleading. Withholding information happens when the suspects makes it difficult for you the lie detector to get the information you require by either hiding of encrypting.

7. Use of faulty poly graph that will lead to bad readings

Even machines are sometimes prone to error, there is a possibility that the readings on a polygraph might be wrong, in fact data has proved that results relayed by polygraphs are usually 80% reliable, What about the other 20%? Also the polygraph interpreter might make some mistakes while interpreting, in some rare suspects have been found guilty of studying and practising how to tune their body reactions when lying with the polygraph attached to them.

8. The suspect claims he needs time to prepare for questioning

Most of the suspects will complain that they are not ready to answer any questions until they have effectively gathered all their information together and also prepared mentally, this will be a challenge to the lie detector especially if they are running on deadlines.

9.   Faulty lie detection techniques

Some of the lie detection techniques might be misinterpreted wrongly and give results that do not reflect on the truth of the matter, this mostly occurs when:

a.   The lie detector does not pay close attention while questioning.

b.   The lie detector was not keen or maybe un-experienced in reading gestures and expressions of the suspect.

VII. Conclusion

Lie detection has been an activity carried out since the beginning of time, until recently did information on how to detect a lie become accessible to the public, in the early days people actually had to use their own instincts and wits to figure out what was going on, the information that has been covered in this book from the first chapter to the last have been verified and adapted by most detectives, lawyers, judges, bosses and so much more of the law enforcers and individuals that are under authority.

How to detect a lie is a process, you will first have to have some first-hand experience in working out this procedures before you venture out to the bigger field, it is basically the same as how a child grows up knowing how to walk.

Detecting a lie using a polygraph is not a hundred per cent guaranteed to give you the right results, also some of the steps mentioned in the book cannot guarantee but will offer you estimation. The more you keep mastering these steps the better you become the lie detection machine.

In some cases it is illegal to conduct lie detecting techniques with no official authority from the government or body in charge that is if the subject matter is delicate or affects the peace or wellbeing of other citizens.